LETTS GUIDES TO
◇ GARDEN DESIGN ◇

Arches & Pergolas

LETTS GUIDES TO
⋄ GARDEN DESIGN ⋄

Arches &
Pergolas

⋄ ROBERT DITCHFIELD ⋄

· CHARLES LETTS · *Letts* of London® · FOUNDED 1796

First published in 1992
by Charles Letts & Co Ltd.
Letts of London House, Parkgate Road
London SW11 4NQ

Edited, designed and produced by
Robert Ditchfield Ltd
Combe Court
Kerry's Gate
Hereford HR2 0AH

ISBN 1 – 85238 – 329 – 1

A CIP catalogue record for this book is available from the British Library.

'Letts' is a registered trademark of Charles Letts & Co Limited

Typeset in Great Britain by Action Typesetting Ltd, Gloucester
Printed and bound in Belgium

ACKNOWLEDGEMENTS

Photographs are reproduced by kind permission of the following:
Robert Ditchfield Ltd (photographer Bob Gibbons): 2, 12, 14, 42, 46;
Andrew Lawson: 7, 17, 23, 27 above (Westwell Manor), 32, 38, 39, 41, 43
(Westwell Manor); W.A. Lord: 9, 10, 19, 22, 25, 36, 40, 47, 50, 51 right, 55, 57;
S & O Matthews: 11, 15, 16, 28, 35. All other photographs are by Diana Saville who
would like to thank the owners of the many gardens in which they were taken,
including Barnsley House, Kiftsgate Court, Lower Hall, The Priory,
Stone House Cottage and Whitfield.

ILLUSTRATIONS

Page 1: Sweet peas on a bamboo frame enliven the vegetable garden.
Frontispiece: Rambler roses are trained over pillars and arches.
Page 5: Ancient topiary yew arch of Italianate design.

CONTENTS

INTRODUCTION

A garden should surround you. Too often it grows only around your ankles, when it should be shoulder-high and above your head, lifting your gaze up to a skyline. Trees are the usual way of developing this vertical dimension in a garden and nothing can replace them. But they are not the only means to hand. Arches, pergolas, tunnels and arbours will all give flowery and leafy ceilings and walls to parts of your garden.

To walk through such a garden means you are not just enfolded by plants but may actually be caressed by their flowers. These ceilings and uprights might be in blossom for only a few weeks of the year, but it becomes an event to anticipate. Days when long trails of white and violet wisteria drift around your head. Or when the most intensely scented roses flower in hanging sprays.

Even when the flowers have died, the foliage on these structures has its own independent value. Walking beneath them, you see the sun through the leaves, giving them a golden translucence and making patterns with their veins. In a large tunnel or pergola, light and shade – those elements we normally take for granted – make their own decoration. Light enters a pergola in rhythmic shafts, bursting

ABOVE: Lonicera periclymenum *'Belgica' on a simple arch.*

OPPOSITE: This decorative gate is topped by a froth of rambler roses, framing the green view beyond.

regularly through the cross-bars overhead, alternating with the shade they cast. In a tunnel, where the light is filtered by foliage, it changes colour, becoming now greenish, now even deep blue and violet in certain atmospheres.

These structures add therefore a genuinely different dimension to a garden. Moreover, it is one that is achieved relatively quickly. A tree will take many years to reach maturity. An arcade or a pergola can be swiftly erected and, provided it is planted with vigorous climbers, can be festooned within a few years. Even a laburnum tunnel, a currently fashionable device in larger gardens, should be showering golden rain along the length of its arches within six years. For a hasty gardener, they ensure the ultimate blessing: the maximum effect within the minimum time.

Wisteria floribunda *mingled with* Clematis montana *'Tetrarose' softens the heavy solidity of th* stone arch.

The History

The contribution made by arches and pergolas to our gardens is not only unique but timeless. Both are of ancient origin and have appeared in a succession of reincarnations in various parts of the world. They have reappeared, festooned with changing plants and built to different forms and sometimes from new materials for more than 4,000 years. China had a tradition of pergolas, which they developed in the form of verandahs. The Japanese devised the enchanting pergola bridge, its curved overhead framework dipping to meet its inverted

reflection in the water to form a flattened circle.

Arches and arbours also existed in the hot sub-tropics of ancient Egypt, that gardened land of pomegranates, fig trees and date palms. Here arches were erected to be productive, for they were used to support vines, but it is evident that they also provided a shaded stroll in even the fiercest sun. Wall paintings in the tomb of a nobleman buried in 1425 BC still show how grapevines were trained over a type of arch.

Then as later, the use of these structures became one of the marks of a civilized and sophisticated society.

Fifteen hundred years on, th pergola, adorned with rose and vines and climbing plants, was an accepted par of wealthier Roman and provincial gardens. Thes were grand, sometimes even vulgar affairs, sporting vaulted arbours as well with wooden roofs and stone pillars, occasionally topped with busts or animal heads.

Much later, in another era linked arches decorated th green and cloistered medieval garden. The earliest and perhaps the grandest to be illustrated was in the *Trè Riches Heures du Duc de Berry*, dated 1489. Here a high vine-clad tunnel surrounded the garden by the royal castle, with corner-joins of high-domed arbours like bird cages.

It is clear that by this time, these devices had become the objects of fantasy and had developed into rich men's toys. The pursuit of their elaboration led to sides of latticework, as in the enchantingly ornamental version displayed in Boccaccio's *Decameron*. By the end of the sixteenth century, these old-fangled charms with their long history had reached England, partly as a result of Henry VIII's despatch of his gardener to the Continent to study Renaissance gardens.

It was in this way that these elegant, elaborate shelters – until now a hot country's defence against a torrid climate – established themselves in the cooler and often rainy climate of the north as well. Pergolas, arches, arbours and tunnels were now ubiquitous.

It was not only the beguiling charms of these structures that earned them such a continuing life. It was also the fact that in cooler climates they were increasingly given a variety of useful and decorative functions. Here they offered not only shade – not always necessary – but, in their many different forms, they acted as simple frames for a view or as garden divisions; they offered protection against wind, they provided decorative walks, and also – a refinement enjoyed by the Tudors who built arbours into their garden corridors – pausing-points for a conversation.

At Giverney, Monet's garden in France, white wisteria provides a romantic canopy to the Japanese-style bridge.

Nowadays, we have continued this imaginative historical tradition, though with our little gardens, we have found it necessary to build them on a more human scale. Placed as a complement to a house, we may use a pergola as a dining-room. Festooned with the scarlet flowers of runner-beans, an arch might adorn our kitchen garden. Weeping with pink robinia, an arcade leads the eye to a seat in the ornamental garden. Twin lines of the domestic apple tree make a gnarled and curved framework for a path. The possibilities are endless which is why these structures have continued to live.

A thick yew doorway straddles the path.

A Frame for a View

Arches and tunnels, which are simply an extended series of related and often actually linked arches, are suitable when you want to direct the eye to a particular focus. A fine seat, for example, or simply an ornament will form an attraction for the eye at the end of a tunnel, implying to the visitor that there is a destination that is worth the effort. Even a simple arch can be used to act as a frame for a feature. The effect it achieves can be dramatic, for it will anchor the feature to its position and emphasize its importance.

THE PURPOSE OF STRUCTURES

Of all the devices that we erect in our gardens, arches and pergolas and their relations look the most romantic; and to the casual garden visitor these structures, festooned by their roses or trailed by wisteria, might appear to be solely decorative. To the gardener, however, they have a practical function, too, as their purpose is to support climbing plants. It is this link between horticulture and ornament that enables pergolas and arches to make a unique contribution to our gardens.

Although pergolas differ from tunnels and arches from arbours, each of these separate structures shares the common characteristic that they add height to a garden. This makes them valuable tools of design. Gardens which are uniformly flat are boring. The eye needs to be lifted at certain points to be diverted.

The height of these structures means that they can be used as devices to grow even tall climbers. Roses which might overshoot their allotted space on the normal wall or fence can be trained up and over a bower. Wisteria which could only be grown as a standard in a tub in a small town garden can be trained along and over a pergola.

Paths

Both tunnels and pergolas developed into shelters for paths. In modern gardens, this means that a path with even the most prosaic purpose – leading from a garage, say, to a house door – can be converted into a most beautiful passage with drifts of flowers or fruit clusters. More elegant destinations, however, deserve superior treatment, even underfoot, which means paying attention to the path itself. Tunnels, in particular, tend to frame the path beneath them as much as the single focus at their end, and a gracefully designed path will be thrown into relief in this position.

Climbing marrows supported by an arcade.

Doorways and Enclosures

As a doorway, the simple arch is the most suitable. Unlike the pergola or tunnel, it may not need a path beneath it, but it still has a function for the stroller, leading him from one area to the next. In this position, it acts as an architrave around an imaginary door, telling you there is a proper transition here, or a start or a finish to a walk. Curiously, this message is at its most emphatic when the archway is simply a vacant space carved out of a hedge. Here it forms a permanently open doorway which entices the visitor to explore the garden on the other side. In a tiny garden, it could even be used as a form of *trompe l'oeil* if the hedge with its open arch is made just before the end of the garden. So long as there is a backcloth of an evergreen like ivy beyond the hedge, the doorway will still appear to be leading elsewhere.

A sense of privacy and enclosure is also very important in gardens. There will be certain areas where you might want to eat quietly and in shade, to sit without feeling exposed. For this purpose, a pergola is ideal, being large enough to accommodate a table and chairs without being cramped or claustrophobic. By contrast, a bower or arbour is usually too small to offer space for more than two people. It can provide a private perch for an afternoon's leisure, but can scarcely be pushed to house a lunch party.

The Rule of Simplicity

It is the very allure of all these structures that leads to their mis-use. These buildings are only appropriate in the right settings. Wrongly positioned, they just litter the ground and clutter the garden. Ensuring that each has a true purpose will be one way of avoiding this unfortunate result. A second measure is to be confident that your structure fits into the style of your garden. Lastly, stick to the rule of simplicity. One type of building is enough in most small gardens and it must be the right one, too.

ABOVE: *An astrolabe is the focus beyond the pink rambling rose 'Débutante' and maroon 'Bleu Magenta'.*

OPPOSITE: Rosa *'Veilchenblau' frames a long perspective.*

THE SIMPLE ARCH

At its simplest an arch can be formed simply by persuading two plants – usually but not necessarily two trees – to link hands overhead. They can be lightly clipped to do so, or you can give them a wooden or metal structure to which they can be tied. But even before you buy or make an arch for any plant, you should be confident that you have the right position for your structure. This is true because an arch which is inconsequentially sited can destroy the logic of your garden.

What are the best positions? You could try using the arch as a doorway, ideally where you cannot see round it: perhaps where you enter a garden, or leave it, or between one area and another. It can sometimes be used effect-ively in the middle of a path where it acts like a piece of elastic, holding the hazy planting on each side together, giving a valuable moment of tension and breaking up a long run without incident. It is equally serviceable used as a frame to a garden 'picture'. This is a theatrical device that tells you what you should look at. 'Stop and admire' is the message – so the focus should be worthwhile as the subject is being forced to pose for the viewer.

When placing the arch you also have to consider what it will do to the rest of your garden. In some contexts it can be too dominant and will alter the balance, perhaps switching the weight to one side rather than another. Is this what the garden needs? Will it need a planting or a structure or a focus of similar weight on the other side to keep it in balance?

Informal or Formal

Your next consideration should be whether your garden requires a formal or informal arch. This is likely to be decided by the position the arch occupies, but your choice must also be governed by the tone of your garden with which the arch should sympathize. All garden buildings, even of the simplest kind, must gel or their presence will be disruptive. In a cottage garden, for example, where excess and show is entirely out of place, a froth of the lovely small-flowered *Clematis viticella* would be an unaffected late summer addition, tossing over a hoop. Or, equally unpretentious, two apple trees could be trained to link over an arch. The merit of this is the simple charm of its mix of Flora and Pomona, flowering in spring, fruiting in autumn.

In complete contrast, the style of a Japanese-influenced garden would dictate an entirely different approach. Here two naturally arching bamboos – possibly *Sinarundinaria murielae* or *Arundinaria nitida* – could be planted either side of a path. Given the concealed support of a roofed arch, they would curve into each other, with their pendent fronds above your head.

RIGHT: Rosa 'Adelaïde d'Orléans' overhead.

OPPOSITE: Two apple cordons in the wild garden.

Materials

It will reduce the possibility of problems in the future if you choose your materials with a view to the plants they must support. For one reason, some plants adapt themselves to square-topped arches made of wood, whilst others don't. For another reason, certain plants are so heavy with foliage and flowers in full growth that the arch must be strong enough to support them.

Metal hoops like an up-turned U are the easiest to buy, obtainable from good garden centres or specialist suppliers. They are better covered by discreetly coloured black or very dark green nylon as naked metal is likely to rust. You can also buy arches made of sawn timber, rustic poles (which rot quite quickly), or trellis-work. In any case, make sure that the arch is wide enough for your purpose. This is particularly important if you are growing thorny roses which can turn the passage through an arch into an incident to be avoided. 4½ft/1.3m is the minimum comfortable width for one person; for two, 7ft/2.1m is essential and 8ft/2.4m is better. One wants to be enclosed but not squeezed, and never scratched. A height of 8ft/2.4m is usual.

RIGHT: Rosa 'Adelaïde d'Orléans' overhead.

Constructing an Arch

If you don't want to buy an arch, it is easy to construct one, though it is likely to be square-topped rather than curved as it is difficult to make your materials flexible without a dedicated workshop. Whilst it is possible to cut a shallow arch out of a softwood board 6in × 6in/15cm × 15cm, such a technique requires the use of a heavy duty jig saw and a grain pattern in the wood that follows the curve of the arch.

A single arch would usually consist of four uprights made from pressure-treated squared softwood, measuring 4in × 4in/10cm × 10cm. These will in effect make two arches placed very close together and linked by horizontal battens for stability. Ideally the wood should be seasoned to prevent deterioration in wet winters. Cross the uprights with 4in × 3in/10cm × 7.5cm overheads for a flat-topped arch and add diagonal braces between the vertical and horizontal timbers.

Planting an Arch

Whether you buy or make the structure, it is essential to plunge it firmly in the ground. When top-heavy with foliage, it is highly vulnerable to wind. The most secure method is to dig a hole of 18in to 2ft/45 to 60cm depth, into which you put the posts and add a concrete mix. Smooth this off just above ground level, sloping the mix from the point of contact with the pole to the ground at the edge of the hole. This will ensure that rain cannot collect around the base of the post. Perfectionists use metal sleeves to protect this vulnerable bottom of the post, but these can look too reminiscent of electricity poles. Whilst it is important to engineer an arch into a long and safe life, it can look unromantic if your methods are too obtrusive.

The Shape

The materials you choose will affect the shape of your arch. Metal makes a genuine arch in that it can be formed into a curved profile. In contrast, thick wooden poles are inflexible: as a result an arch constructed out of these will be a misnomer, as it must be a flat-topped rectangle or square. When smothered with flowers, this rigidity of outline will be lost, but its right-angle shape does confine you to growing plants with pliable stems, like rambler roses. It is a fact that either the plant must bend to the arch or the arch to the plant. In gardening as in life: a prolonged partnership involves a high degree of compromise.

When you are choosing the shape of an arch which is being used as a garden 'picture frame', you might bear in mind that an object with a curved outline can look at its best when captured in a square frame. Conversely a focal point which has rectangular proportions is softened when seen through a curving viewpoint. This is true whether the perspective is short or long. In a formal garden, it is this careful match of detail, these tight links between shape of arch, plant and its focus, that will make everything look satisfyingly predestined, not thoughtless and random which would spoil it.

ABOVE: *Rambler roses festoon an arcade.*

RIGHT: *Colour-coordinated arcade and borders in a far-reaching view.*

THE ARCADE

*A*n arch turns into an arcade by multiplying itself into a series of parallel arches. Does this make it a tunnel? Not in the context of a garden. An arcade differs from a tunnel (see page 34) because it is relatively open overhead and within. Tunnels are enclosed and claustrophobic devices, temporarily obliterating the outside world. Arcades are airy and your surroundings – the sky and garden views – are part of your outlook when you walk along their length.

Although an arcade is not necessarily grander than the simple arch, it is more obvious, so needs even more careful positioning than its little relative. It must, for example, cover a path. It must start from a logical point and reach a serious destination. And it shouldn't throw the garden off-balance.

The arcade differs too from the single arch in that it is not a momentary experience as you pass through. As an area of transition, it prolongs your experience. It takes you on a journey, defining at length (and restricting) where you walk. It is therefore always a more formal feature than an arch and requires a more formal setting and a rather larger one. If each arch is spaced at an interval of about 10ft/3m (this is optional and the distance can vary between 8ft/2.4m and 15ft/4.6m), it can occupy a considerable space. Finally, at the very least, the arcade can only be included in flat gardens (or flat areas of the garden). A sloping arcade would give a comically insecure appearance.

So far, the arcade sounds like a pergola, and it is not surprising there is confusion between the two structures. Whilst an arcade shares the same function as a pergola – both are used as corridors – it differs in its shape and its effect. It is always constructed with a curved top (a pergola has a square-topped

roof') and has a more graceful unified profile. Whilst this delicacy of line is an advantage in many garden settings, it means that the structure may not support the same weight of plants as the stout architectural type of pergola.

When you are trying to choose between the merits of arcades, tunnels and pergolas for your garden, you might consider that arcades have a special advantage. They don't drip as much. Close overhead planting on a structure can be a nuisance in wet climates for it will continue to shed water even after the rain has stopped. An arcade which is formed of widely spaced and unconnected single hoops will be less of a problem in this respect.

Finally one can even make an arcade out of hedging shrubs, like the hornbeam in the photograph on page 57. On a lesser scale, this could be appropriate in even a small formal garden. Highly controlled and architectural, it could take a decade to achieve and its arches would be demanding to clip, but the effect is impressive.

PLANTING THE ARCH

shade into account unless it is erected in a dark position (which will restrict your choice of plants). It is therefore simple to plant.

Roses are a first favourite, scoring highly because they are billowy and pretty from a distance yet rewarding to view and smell at close quarters. Weak-stemmed roses are no disadvantage over an arch for their nodding blossoms will look towards you. For this reason, 'Adelaïde d'Orléans' is a good choice with her weeping creamy blush flower heads which have been likened to cherry-blossom. But the later-flowering white 'Aimée Vibert' or the sumptuous maroon 'Bleu Magenta' or the clustering pink 'Débutante' are all very beautiful. The snag is that these flower only once and the recurrent silvery-pink 'New Dawn' or the white 'Climbing Iceberg' may be preferred for their continuity.

Honeysuckles can be combined with roses to make a scented arch – for example, the faded blue-mauve 'Veilchenblau', with its light sweet smell, and the yellow *Lonicera periclymenum* 'Graham Thomas', a cultivar of the hedgerow honeysuckle.

Clematis, too, can be chosen either to flower at the same time as the rose, which will reinforce your effects, or to give a separate performance and thereby provide a longer season of show. For the first purpose, you might plant the buff-yellow rose 'Easlea's Golden Climber'

The single arch can only support one or at most two plants to pretty effect, so the choice matters. The plants need to flower at the right time for the garden and at the right height for the arch. The ultimate size of the climbers (and your pruning may govern this – see page 60), colour, period of flowering and degree of recurrence should all be suitable.

An arch makes its effect in a different way from a pergola, arcade or tunnel, because it is viewed solely from without rather than within. It has virtually no interior, so you need not take

ABOVE: *Arcade of roses in Monet's garden at Giverney, France.*

OPPOSITE: *Rosa 'Veilchenblau' partnered with honeysuckle over an arch.*

with the mauve-blue clematis 'Ascotiensis' over a big arch; or the silvery-pink 'New Dawn' with the maroon-velvet clematis 'Niobe'. Or, to achieve separate effects, try the rose 'Blush Noisette' for its palest pink showers (it is recurrent though its true flush is in high summer) and follow it with the double dusky purple *Clematis viticella* 'Purpurea Plena Elegans'.

An arch of this kind will be ravishing during its summer performance and quiet but unobtrusive in leaf when it is resting. Between times it can look a fright. Most very double roses are ugly when they die as the browning petals cling to the stem. This

can be especially apparent with pale-coloured rosettes so avoid these if they will spoil your neighbouring effects – unless you are willing to dead-head. Winter is the other off-season, when only a tangle of stems and shoots are apparent. In a highly formal garden, it might be better to opt for an arch made by sculptured plants (see overleaf) or choose for your arch a good dense ivy-covering – a suitable cultivar would be 'Manda's Crested'. This can be kept clipped to shape and you could grow a late-flowering clematis over this. You can cut the latter to near the ground in late winter/early spring.

Planting Arcades

The thrill of an arcade is that it gives you much more scope for planting than a single arch. You can swag it with rows of roses, garlands of clematis, combining their colours not simply on the arch they adorn, but over the succession of archs that form the whole structure. One could treat such a scheme virtually as a border, planning colour crescendos so long as they respected the context of the garden. And where the legs of the arcade are planted into flower borders on either side, it is in effect part of that border, spanning and relating its colour and texture.

CLIPPED ARCHES

A rches are at their most successful when formed from hedges. In this context they are virtually topiary for they are sculptured from plants. They are no mere ornament, however, but have a purpose – to act as a doorway in a wall or to form a pediment over an existing gap in a hedge. They therefore provide the ideal opportunity to unite function and decoration.

They are also much more easily integrated into a setting than the isolated arch or arcade. After all, they are part of a garden's structure as the hedge from which they grow forms its very bones. This doesn't give a licence to place them anywhere along a hedge. You still have to decide, first, which kind of hedge is appropriate for treatment, and, second, the right point at which to make your arch.

The sort of hedge which lends itself best to any overhead or slightly inaccessible topiary is one which needs minimum clipping. A once-a-year-job is your aim. This means that a hedge of the fast-growing *Cupressus × leylandii* or *Lonicera nitida* is out. Yew (*Taxus baccata*) or *Thuja occidentalis* are better possibilities. These are dense evergreens so your arch will do equal service in winter. Although it is equally attractive to exploit the deciduous hornbeam, beech etc. in the same way (other options are listed on page 56), their arches will suffer a seasonal eclipse.

LEFT: *A free-standing arch of Sorbus aria 'Lutescens' – the climax of rose borders.*

OPPOSITE: *A yew arch forms a sober backcloth to foaming twin herbaceous borders.*

Forming the Arch

A free-standing arch of sculptured plants can be formed by planting one shrub outside each leg of a frame, keeping its side shoots trimmed and growing its young pliable stem up and over the frame until it meets its opposite number. Alternatively, without a frame, simply clip side shoots to form an archway between the shrubs, allowing those overhead to join up. When an arch is part of a hedge, it is formed in the same way as topiary (details of training are given on page 60).

In either case, the arch is best in sun, for a perfect clipped shrub will not grow evenly in part-shade. It will also risk injury if exposed to scourging wind and cold. This is true even when it is part of a hedge, for it projects above the hedge and above its own micro-climate. This and the fact that regular clipping robs it of its outer coat of wind-filtering and cold-protecting shoots makes it vulnerable. The solution is to give your sculptured arch a sheltered situation and always select bone-hardy plants if severe winters are a problem in your region.

Siting the Arch

Where do you site the arch? You judge this by the same criteria as for the simple, single arch. It should be placed where it will signify an entrance or an exit, or, perhaps, a change of garden 'room'. It could serve equally well as a severe frame for a flowery view. You can make great play with contrasts here: a yew arch, for example, could be an exercise in sobriety, framing a particularly ebullient, frothy planting ahead.

This kind of contrast is even better in reverse, where foaming herbaceous borders either side of a path can be given a full stop in the form of a dark clipped arch beyond. You can even make a deliberate colour scheme out of the arch and its foreground. The silvery whitebeam, *Sorbus aria* 'Lutescens', is the climax to which the twin rose borders lead in the photograph, above. This is an example of an isolated arch – and since it is not integrated into the hedge either side, its integration in this case is solely with its foreground.

TRIPODS, SCREENS AND POLES

In addition to arches and pergolas, there are other structures you can use for height in your garden. Indeed, where space is at a premium, you may prefer slimmer props that need less *lebensraum*. Some of these are portable devices that can be repositioned in different years, though they should always be integrated in the garden rather than seeming incidental.

Tripods, pyramids, decorative screens and even a simple pole with a mesh surround can all be pressed into service. Although they provide neither shade nor overhead cover, they will direct the eye or punctuate a border or separate one area of the garden from another. A screen can act as the hasty man's hedge – it is even a preferable alternative as it takes less space and doesn't come with the curse of greedy, invasive roots. This structure isn't so easy to reposition, however, as it must be very firmly plunged in the ground if it is to be a secure support for plants.

These props may or may not be garden furniture, by which I mean features that are intended to be ornamental as well as functional. If unequivocally decorative, you will want to avoid smothering them completely with plants. Unfortunately, they can look a bit self-conscious when naked. One answer is to use structures like ornamental tripods as supports for annual climbers. This way, they will be temporarily covered. Even sweet peas, usually abandoned to twigs and twine, can look very pretty over these. You could try a blend of colour for each tripod, or, if you have three or more of these structures, a lovelier option would be to have a different colour for each: cream, then mauve, followed by violet, and possibly indigo.

RIGHT: *Sweet peas and Clematis 'Perle d'Azur' grow over a tripod.*

OPPOSITE: *Garlands of pink roses trail like necklaces to form a screen.*

Priorities

You also have to decide which has priority – the prop or the plant – and then match the satellite to the star. Climbing roses, for example, are at their most graceful grown up posts and then trailed in a necklace along linking ropes or chains, though the latter can chafe. It is not only their flexibility that makes them ideal for this purpose, but their habit of flowering too: trained horizontally, they will blossom along the length of their stem. It is these characteristics of the plants that point the way to a suitable method of display and the logical prop to achieve this. Bear in mind, however, that this method is flamboyant and formal and not for every garden.

Clematis, being opportunist scramblers, are best grown over a mesh support on a pillar. This looks down-at-heel before it is covered by plants, and a smarter alternative is a spherical metal structure called a balloon. So long as the pillar or pole is tall enough, this can be highly effective in a border, giving a lift to a plant which lacks its own means of support.

You can adapt the height of the pole to the plant: *Hydrangea petiolaris*, for example, can be used to cover a support of virtually any reasonable height and is dense and sturdy enough to include in a shrub border.

Roses are also sometimes grown over pillars, but are best trained to wind round them; this helps to distribute the sap along the stem and to encourage evenly distributed flowers. Even if grown one to each leg of a tall tripod, this form of training secures the best results.

Virginia creeper (Parthenocissus quinquefolia) on an architectural pergola.

PERGOLAS

Pergolas of whatever size and materials conform to a simple pattern. They are made out of a series of linked squares or rectangles. Indeed, formality as well as geometry is their keynote, for they are – or should be – permanent and must never look flimsy or ephemeral. They are also potentially spectacular for the stoutest type of pergola can support the noblest climber we can grow: the wisteria in its many varieties and colours.

Though the pergola may assume a grand or more humble guise, it is in its architectural form that it is the most magnificent of garden buildings. This was the kind of structure that adorned the more illustrious ancient gardens, as in Egypt where brick supports supplanted wooden uprights. Correspondingly, it was this imposing type of structure that became so popular in the great gardens of Italy. Here massive columns of stone were customarily used and made ornate and important pergolas.

In England, the Edwardian era was the heyday of the architectural pergola. Here the great exponent of this type of corridor was the architect, Sir Edwin Lutyens though he was typically innovative on an old theme. He alternated brick with stone pillars, for example and at Marsh Court, his *chef d'oeuvre* in Surrey, he erected pillars of tiles stacked with a wide mortar bed between each and keyed the slightly arched cross-beams overhead into the house wall. Gertrude Jekyll, the designer with whom Lutyens worked favoured this use of arched cross-beams, particularly when partnered with a further refinement: a concave brace supporting the join between upright and cross-beam.

Hestercombe, the garden in Somerset on which Lutyens worked with Jekyll, contained another masterly pergola. Here he alternated round with square uprights, thus helping to break the monotony of a very long run of 240ft/72m. He used local stone for the pillars and oak for the cross-beams which were subtly cambered. In almost every respect, it exemplified Jekyll's advice that 'the upward curve, if even quite slight, gives a satisfying look of strength'. (Her perception was right, for straight cross-beams can often give the illusion of sagging in the middle.) It was this kind of delicate treatment that brought garden ornament to the most perfect maturity.

These monuments – examples of the classic or grand pergola – were devised at a time when

A wooden pergola of roses at the formal garden of Bagatelle, France.

architects dominated the garden. They made such substantial masses that they could be accommodated only in the kind of powerfully architectural and formal environment that spawned them. One big enough, moreover, to take the reduction in space from this kind of furniture.

Few modern gardens could house them nowadays, but a larger than average garden might be suitable for a smaller, lightweight version, so long as it would not be dominated by the structure. Any such building would

also have to be very carefully positioned. In this respect, one rule of thumb is that you should increase the architectural character of a pergola as it nears the house.

For those with the space, choice and purse to accommodate the architectural pergola, it is worth noting that length of run will truly exploit its best characteristics. Only when you walk beneath a long pergola can you appreciate the rhythmic shafts of alternating light and shade. Or the telescopic illusion as you look towards the far end. Neither of these

pleasures is in store, if the pergola is either too short or too narrow.

These principles of the classic and grand pergola might seem irrelevant to today's gardener with a smallish plot, but anyone who builds a pergola should take them into account. Even a lightweight pergola will need to be long enough and wide enough to justify its site and purpose. Most important of all, the lesson to be learned from the classic pergola is that it formed part of the overall concept of the garden. It was appropriate.

Positioning Pergolas

Bewitching as the pergola is, it comes with the caveat that it is not for sloping gardens nor for those in areas of high rainfall, where it will be in a perpetual state of drip. And even in a garden perfectly suited to it, you have to position the pergola correctly.

This is especially true of the architectural pergola which cannot blend unobtrusively into the garden, unlike its more rustic wooden counterpart; and a pergola that fails to fit in is a very obvious intrusion indeed. A few general rules may be useful. Firstly, an architectural pergola is usually at its best near a house, where it can conform to its building materials, whether brick or stone. Next, as a formal structure, it needs to be placed over a formal path or paved area which it will cover. In addition, it ought to have starting- or finishing-points of importance, and the house or a garden building might well form one end.

Alternatively, the pergola could be anchored on one side to a wall where its cross-beams and uprights – the equivalent of a builder's joists and timbers – are truly at home. If the wall belongs to the house or its immediate surrounds, the pergola takes the place of a verandah and will form a green, shady and private dining-room. Here it is not a transitional but a static feature and can be planted like a garden room.

Materials may be architectural or rustic, but in either case it is essential that the structure looks attractive when naked – especially if it is in full view of the house. It is all too easy to erect a pergola which looks ravishing in its summer drapery of climbers and dismal when bare of foliage in winter.

The Architectural Pergola

The materials you use will depend on the context. Architectural pergolas can be constructed of the same materials as the house. Otherwise architectural salvage merchants could be a possible source for columns: these might be suitable so long as they don't evoke the Parthenon.

An ingenious substitute is shown in the garden in the photograph on the opposite page (below, right). Here 4in/10cm concrete drainpipes form the uprights and are crossed with elm battens. Embowered in vines and clematis, it forms an elegant structure, transforming the materials completely from their original character. In fact, any concrete irrigation tube can serve the same purpose, but for stability they should be filled with reinforcement rods and concrete.

In a hot climate metal poles are an unsuitable option. They can absorb so much heat from the sun that they will scorch the plants you grow over them. The same is true of modern scaffolding poles which are sometimes

used as uprights and with softwood horizontals overhead, treated with preservative. Again, if the metal overheats in summer, your plants will suffer. You can leave these structures unplanted, but they will look hideously utilitarian and will also be useless for privacy.

ABOVE: Wisteria floribunda 'Macrobotrys' in a perfect partnership with a strong architectural pergola. Note the seat within.

RIGHT: Elegant and ingenious – concrete pipes and wooden battens are draped with Vitis vinifera purpurea and clematis.

Wooden Pergolas

In many gardens, the light effect of the wooden pergola will be more suitable than its architectural counterpart. For these, softwood poles are normally used though they have to be pressure-treated with preservative for durability. Even then, they are sometimes sunk in drainpipes in concrete (sealed at the top to prevent rain penetrating between pole and pipe).

For a rustic air, larchwood used to be favoured with the bark left on; but barked wood is so prone to decay and can look so amateurish that, if you can afford it, squared beams (6-9in/15-22.5cm) are the better option. They have a more substantial appearance, especially if they are given 'feet', the planted or constructed equivalent of plinths or piers. These will give visual stability to any up-

right, whether brick, stone or wood. As with the architectural pergola, ingenuity can inspire a source of supply. In one garden I know, the owners had the bright idea of using defunct electricity poles for the uprights.

Occasionally split bamboo fencing is laid across as a roof but it won't last for much more than a summer. Nor does it offer the slightest support for climbers. It is

ABOVE: Wood and brick pergola grows from a building.

OPPOSITE: Simple wooden pergola with roses and a floor of petals.

Measurements

In 1933 a standard textbook was published called *Landscape Gardening – Planning – Construction – Planting*. It was written by Richard Sudell, a leading garden designer before the war. His entry on the pergola has influenced garden designers ever since and its good sense is still valid today. It has saved many pergolas from being too short and too narrow.

The opposite uprights should be 8ft/2.4m apart. By the time they are festooned with climbers, which will take up quite a bit of space themselves, this will be none too wide. I would add a rider that if you intend to plant in a ribbon bed on either side of the path within the pergola, then this spacing may need to be further still.

The uprights should also be spaced at 8ft/2.4m intervals along the pathway. These pillars, whatever their material, need to be plunged firmly in the ground, ideally in 18in or 2ft/45 or 60cm concrete footings, leaving 8 – 10ft/2.4 – 3m above the ground.

The runners – namely, the continuous timber beams which extend along each side of the pergola – should be 6 × 4in/15 × 10cm. 4in/10cm square crossbars which join onto the runners over the pillars, usually complete the frame with projecting ends, often moulded. A pergola of this nature will be open enough to produce rhythmic bursts of light and shade in its interior. But it can be turned into a completely shady tunnel if you add longitudinal battens of wood to encourage climbing plants to grow overhead. However, more wood means a greater work-load. Preservative has only a limited life and the punctilious owner needs to apply it regularly (using a brand that cannot harm plants).

only a temporary – and expensive for that reason – means of giving you shade until your plants can perform the same function. Trellis is a rather more permanent optional extra for overhead, and it is sometimes used as an infill along the sides. Here it will add extra support for climbing stems and make the pergola rather more of an enclosure and a divider.

29

Planting the Pergola

Planting a pergola is one of the purest pleasures of gardening, but you may decide to restrain the impulse somewhat. Some pergolas are better left partially free. No one would want to obscure completely structures that are highly ornamental, whereas many wooden erections look much the better for a full-blooded smothering.

Whatever the context you also have to decide whether to go for a brief period of brilliance or whether to eek out the effects with long-flowering climbers or plants that bloom successively. With the latter, you have to plan more carefully, but are rewarded by long-term blossom which may be equally as dramatic as the first option. Whatever your preference, the best effects come from simplicity and consistency in planting, whether in foliage or colour.

Fruit on Pergolas

One of the best choices is to opt for weeping fruit or flowers: they are the best suited to this position for the obvious reason that they hang down or turn their blossoms to face you inside your pergola. Vines, the original pergola-covering, are still among the loveliest and the most useful whether for vigour of growth, density of covering or controllability. The effect they provide from within (and the interior is at least as important as the

Cottage garden pergola with braces at the junction of uprights and crossbars. It is closely carpeted with flowers which integrate it into the garden.

outside in a pergola) is enchanting, sunlight irradiating the intensely green leaves and the burgundy or golden jewelled bunches of fruit. *Vitis vinifera* 'Brandt', with black grapes, is an especially good form as the autumn colouring of its leaves is intensely red and gold.

Other fruit has also been used in the past, even gourds. This sounds bizarre but the round turbanned kind of fruit is not unsuited to so artificial a form of display; grown early as a tender annual, it could form a fill-in for the first summer after building the pergola when it would otherwise look bare.

Hydrangea arborescens *makes a lolling white bank in shade by a pergola.*

Flowers on Pergolas

Most people, however, would opt for flowers not fruit. Wisteria remains unequalled, especially *Wisteria floribunda* (though the form 'Macrobotrys' with its 3ft/90cm trails may be inconveniently long). It has grace, mass of leaf, a spectacular season of bloom and the pendulous tresses that are so at home in the pergola. Other possibilities include the orange-red *Campsis × tagliabuana* 'Madame Galen' for hot areas where its flowering in late summer will be more reliable; *Jasminum officinale* for scent though its flowers are not exactly showy; or the madly floriferous purple *Solanum crispum* 'Glasnevin' which has a very long season of graceful bloom.

For shadier spots, clematis are excellent, especially the *C. viticella* varieties which are resistant to wilt: and also honeysuckles which are less likely to succumb to aphids in a shady position with air round their heads. *Aristolochia durior* with its huge green leaves would do a complete foliage blanket job.

Roses on Pergolas

Roses are arguably more suitable for arches than pergolas. Few have good leaves as well as good flowers, which are essential for a plant candidate here as the structure of a pergola is so stout and dominant that it needs assertive plants as companions. Also a whole run of roses, artificially trained as they are in this position, might be a little cloying in their sweetness. They also have other disadvantages. Many short pillar roses, which will clothe the uprights effectively instead of overshooting the mark like some ramblers, have an unyielding habit of growth. Another drawback is that the flowering season of many roses is either brief and without weeping fruit to follow. Or it is usually intermittent, few beautiful cultivars equalling their first flush.

I am afraid there is one other disadvantage, too. Many rose blossoms are ugly as they die – sadly true of the double white or pink cultivars. This won't matter in a border where you can dead-head them; it is out of the question on a pergola.

However, rose enthusiasts will ignore all this, and some roses transcend these snags anyway. One of these is the climbing form of 'Iceberg' with its great white trusses of double blooms (it doesn't die too badly), produced over a long season. Another is the double silvery-pink 'New Dawn'. This is justifiably popular as it has very healthy shining foliage, the pliant habit of a rambler though it is classified as climber because of its recurrent flowering and, not least, a very fresh scent sometimes likened to apples. Moving to stronger colours, 'Parkdirektor Riggers' is also recurrent and the richness of even a few of its crimson velvet blooms against the leaves is valuable.

The shorter pillar roses which are mentioned on pages 46-7 would be suitable if you only want them to clothe the uprights. They won't vault overhead. And for those who are happy with only a short season of bloom from their roses, there are plenty of subjects recommended on pages 44-7.

LEFT: *Skilful planting ensures an enchanting interior.*

Planning the Display and Underplanting

It is difficult when using a variety of plants as cover for a pergola to avoid incoherence. Though you will get colour and eventfulness throughout the season when you use lots of successional plants, you will also invite messiness unless you plan. One solution is to keep to a single colour. A large pergola could be wondrously festooned from spring until autumn with white-flowered plants.

Training has to be especially strict if you are including different varieties of plants. Wisteria, for example, is so powerful a twiner that it will easily kill its companions unless kept under control. Not only pruning at the right time is required. Lots of tying up is needed too. Training of most plants is easier if you enclose the upright of the pergola with wide-gauge netting to which the plant stems can be tied – an eyesore out of season.

There are two arguments for underplanting the pergola. Firstly you can make glorious combinations between the climbers and those at their feet. Secondly, when the season of brief-flowering climbers is over, you can focus anew on the underplanting. In either case, intimate planting of this type will decorate the interior like a room.

Your choice will depend on the degree of shade that the pergola throws, but it is unlikely that plants which need open sunny conditions will thrive here. However, many of the most beautiful love dappled shade, including a high proportion of campanulas, Japanese anemones, astrantias, and hardy geraniums which will give a range of blues, pinks, mauves and whites. For sculptural perfection, put scented lilies in pots under pergolas. There are many easy-going hybrids which are suitable for pot work, as well as species like *Lilium regale* for high summer and *L. speciosum* for late summer to autumn.

Bulbs which bloom in spring are also ideal beneath a pergola that is covered in deciduous climbers. They will absorb sufficient sunshine to flower and make growth before the canopy becomes excessively dark. Narcissi, or tulips and alliums in the more sunshiny patches will take on an intensity of colour in this cloistered setting.

LEFT: *Gnarled old apple trees have grown into a tunnel over a path.*

OPPOSITE: *The glorious laburnum tunnel with its mauve alliums in late spring. The shady interior makes the gold and lilac harmonize; in comparison the colours would look harsh together in full sun.*

the goal at its end that save the tunnel from the inevitable failure that results when the structure is left to free-float in the middle of an area without a purpose.

The tunnel formed of single-railed arches provides a training framework for the plants which will soon take over and swamp the railings with their own identity. Unlike the pergola which is often dressed with different plants to form a varied hanging garden, the tunnel tends to be clothed with one kind of plant only. It forms an integrated entity which usually dominates its own area.

As a design-feature, one of its great virtues is that it is flexible enough to be on the simplest scale for the small garden, or on the grandest for highly ambitious schemes. One example of the latter is a garden containing high arches forming tunnels as a surround. These are punctuated at intervals by tall conversational bowers that invite a lingering pause. Scaled down, this could work in even the smaller garden.

TUNNELS

*L*ike the pergola, the tunnel makes an area of transition. It takes you from Somewhere to Somewhere and out from shade into sunlight. It differs from the pergola in that it has a curved apex made out of a series of arches, softer in effect than its right-angled relative.

Nonetheless the resemblances between the two types of structure are stronger than the differences.

Like the pergola, the tunnel should cover a path and transport you to a destination which could be simply a seat to act as an incentive. It is this path and

Framework and Plants

Tunnels are most commonly used as the framework for the vigorous *Laburnum* × *watereri* 'Vossii', the form of laburnum with the longest racemes. Here it will weep its pendulous golden tresses within, where their brash colour will be softened and enhanced by the shade of the interior. Most tunnels are no wider than the pergola, but a laburnum tunnel is improved by increasing the width, which ensures maximum 'weeping' of the trails within. At the National Trust garden of Bodnant in Wales, for example, the laburnum tunnel is 15ft/4.6m wide, the supporting arches spaced at 12ft/3.7m (linked by longitudinal rails) – and it is also about 80yd/74m long. This last measurement has little application to gardens nowadays, but the first two guarantee a rich, flamboyant and potent effect. One, admittedly, that lasts for only two weeks, as laburnum is singularly dull for the remaining fifty weeks of the year.

The razzmatazzy laburnum is not the only candidate and tunnels have been formed with many different plants since their forbears which carried vines. The kind of plant you choose will affect where you plant your tunnel (and vice-versa) for its grouped presence is a dominant one.

Wisterias, whitebeams, yew and even magnolias have all been used. The latter makes a most covetable tunnel. In one garden, six trees of *Magnolia* × *soulangeana* 'Lennei' (a form with long pliable branches bearing deep rose goblets in spring) have been trained over eight iron arches which are spaced 6ft/1.8m from each other. The length of the tunnel is about 20yd/18m with a gentle turn in its destination so that you proceed somewhat mysteriously, being unable to see through to the end. It is a unique and elysian experience for the visitor.

Every available shoot and branch of the six magnolias was tied over and along the arches. As a result the coverage has grown surprisingly sumptuous and complete. Although this kind of magnolia is expensive to buy in the first place, it is fast-growing and its use in this particular situation economical.

RIGHT: Patterns of sunlight on the ground reflect the overhead lattice.

OPPOSITE: Even in winter, this lime tunnel makes dense walls. But note the frustrating effect of the cul-de-sac at the far end.

Fruit Tunnels

The apple or pear tunnel is usually formed by planting cordon fruit trees on semi-dwarfing MM106 rootstock at both feet of each arch, spaced at about 2½ft/ 75cm apart. This intensive planting is not cheap; it also demands strict training and systematic attention if the plants are to fruit well. Details are given on page 60. A cheaper way of covering a fruit tunnel is to grow the trees trained as espaliers along the sides of the arches and then spread their branches along battens that connect the arches; they will form a large enclosed tunnel.

In flower and, even more, in ripened fruit, all fruit tunnels make charming showcases. They can also be highly productive and will take the place of an orchard in a very small garden. Here a simple five hoop tunnel 10ft/3m long would support ten cordons.

These make permanent features. Climbing vegetables can make enchanting temporary alternatives. Marrows, scarlet runner beans or inedible gourds grown solely for decoration can be trained to climb over the hoops, one to each leg of an arch. Great fun, and the beans especially are easier to pick since you can reach them from both sides.

Tree Tunnels

Trees planted closely together, whether pleached or left comparatively free-growing can be encouraged to form a type of avenue or a tunnel. Hornbeam, beech or lime are normally used for pleaching, a method of training whereby branches are spread horizontally on wires and clipped to encourage twiggy offshoots. Lime is popular because it is so flexible. Hornbeam which is often used for the stilt hedge (so-called because the hedge is trained at the top of the trunk) is much cheaper but needs to be of uniform growth. Some hornbeams are weeping and it is a waste to suppress this pretty form by clipping it. Beech makes a lovely rufous hedge in winter as the dead leaves persist on the tree, but can be subject to disease on heavy wet soils.

ARBOURS

*A*n arbour or bower is the most romantic indulgence in a garden, for you are planning for yourself as much as your plants. It adds a cool retreat, intimate, perhaps secret as arbours have been associated with amorous pursuits in the past. Here you can sit, shaded in summer and sheltered at all times, like a mollusc in your shell.

Arbours are also easily accommodated. No more than plants on a canopy, they can be pushed into a sunshiny nook between two walls so that your back is warmed and supported and you can look out over an engaging view. An arch like a rib-vault here,

at its simplest with four ends to be driven into the ground, will give you a domed roof which you can festoon with plants. Alternatively you can buy an eight-legged, ogee-roofed frame in an elegant Gothic style. There are even self-assembly structures on the market which allow you to form arbours of different sizes to which you can apply side panels.

Most of these are of nylon coated metal, but wood may be your preferred option. In this case you could build a little arbour-gallery with trellis at the sides in the manner of Renaissance lattice-work. The great virtue of unpainted wood is that it fades to a quiet mouse colour which is an admirable blender with the plants that cover it in summer, and looks unobtrusive in winter. Arbours of other materials can look rather too demonstrative and it would be wise to pick one in black or dark green rather than white if you have a plastic-coated frame.

White-painted Victorian-style arbour with back support from a brick wall. The ivy has been allowed to grow not only above it but within, erasing the division between building and plants. As it is an evergreen, it will also help to clothe the arbour in winter.

The airiness of the open design makes this free-standing rose arbour almost a summerhouse.

Arbours of Plants

You don't of course have to erect a serious structure for an arbour, but can make a free-standing one out of a weeping tree such as the tall ash, *Fraxinus excelsior* 'Pendula' or the white mulberry, *Morus alba* 'Pendula', the latter so trailing that it has to be staked up if you want to give it height. Both are fine trees though the former is far too big for the average garden and neither, admittedly, is a quick solution for the normal gardener who moves house at quite frequent intervals. But for those who can stay and wait, it is more satisfying and beautiful in the long run, which is a tale of patience rewarded.

A quicker option is to train hornbeams, pleaching them to form a type of stilt hedge around you and a canopy overhead. If you buy them as small standards, they will provide good coverage within a few years, though it will take longer to form the canopy above as the top branches need to grow tall to reach over. Depending on the size of the arbour, five trees will be ample. For training, sufficient framework can be given with strong wires or bamboo stakes to which your chosen leaders from the trees can be tied. Prune the side-shoots as firmly as you would a hedge, to ensure maximum density of coverage. However, leave the leaders which will make the overhead canopy to grow on to the required amount. As they develop, continue to prune their side shoots as above.

39

A sumptuous rose bower formed out of linked arches.

Bowers of Climbers

The way you choose to be embowered might seem a purely personal matter. I once built a very steamy number, coiffured it with bougainvillea and filled it with epiphytic orchids (I *was* in East Africa). It wasn't, however, a total success, and indeed the trouble with most arbours is that their early splurge of perfection is rapidly followed by senile decay. This is sometimes due to an over-flimsy structure, but the plants can be equally at fault. The truth is that few climbers are suitable and even the traditional festooners have their problems.

Honeysuckles, for example, may give you trouble if the site of the structure is against them. A shady arbour will suit them, but a sunny one near hot walls won't. In this position, honeysuckles (whether or not they have their heads in freely cirulating air) are liable to become infested with aphids. Spraying an arbour against pests and diseases is tricky as some parts can be out of easy reach. Besides, it is planned as an area of quiet relaxation rather than strife.

To be embowered in pendent roses is a potent image, but this too may suffer in reality. The vigour of some is a problem for a small bower; the flowering period can be disappointingly brief and you don't have the room to plant lots of successional flowering-plants; also, most roses are thorny which can make a bower a rather challenging place in which to sit.

But if bowers seems synonymous with roses, you could choose the repeat-flowering old climbers like 'Aimée Vibert' with sprays of small white double flowers. Or 'Blush Noisette' with even prettier clusters of lilac-pink rosettes with a rich scent. Shorter growers among modern varieties include 'New Dawn', silver-pink and healthy, and 'Climbing Iceberg' with voluptuous full white blossoms. 'Seagull' will smother you with showers of white flowers. And the old climbing Bourbon rose, 'Zéphirine Drouhin', a rather harsh deep pink has the virtue of being scented and thornless. Her sport, 'Kathleen Harrop' is a gentler pink tint.

Vines

Vines will provide you with a quieter life in an arbour – which is what it is there for – and smother it with foliage. The purple-leafed vine, *Vitis vinifera purpurea*, is slower-growing than most other vines and therefore likely to succeed. Though late into leaf, it earns its keep till autumn, its first pigment of pale olive green gradually turning to ruby and finally to blackish-purple. By late summer, it is studded with trailing clusters of black grapes, too bitter to eat raw, but delicious as a jelly. (Cook them with a cinammon stick and the jelly will taste rich, smoky and mulled.) Like all pendent fruit and flowers, the grapes look lovely from inside the arbour diverting the sitter within.

If pendent flowers have more instant appeal than fruit, you might prefer *Robinia hispida* 'Rosea'. This cultivar is invariably grafted as it suckers on its own roots. In leaf and flower it resembles a wisteria but with stubbier, rich rose-pink racemes which blossom in summer but with a few more in autumn. Unlike a wisteria, it is not rampant and lends itself to being trained over a framework, its stem supported by a stake. It is, with much justification, due to become highly fashionable and its rosy flowers will be seen trailing over many a fortunate head.

The simplest of rose arbours above a seat – a bouffant head-dress in summer.

Clematis for Later Bloom

The beautiful *Clematis viticella* varieties are later-flowering options. These are vigorous but manageable, flexible enough to lead over wires to give you an airy but dense covering of leaves, almost ferny in some varieties, and flowering with abandon from late summer often until autumn. 'Abundance' has a cloud of wine-red butterflies; 'Alba Luxurians' white ones, often green tipped, in a delicate mass. 'Kermesina' has slightly larger blooms of claret velvet, whilst *C.v.* 'Purpurea Plena Elegans' is tremendously floriferous in sun or shade.

Like 'Royal Velours' which is a rich velvet purple, the depth and subtlety of its colouring benefits from a pale background. A crude contrast would dull their beauty, a softer one emphasize it, such as the silvery *Artemisia* 'Powis Castle' or the grey *Buddleja crispa* trained on a sheltered wall nearby which will help this rather tender species.

These clematis need to be cut down in early spring; though, to extend their flowering season, you can cut half down then and the other half a month later. Full pruning details of these and other clematis varieties are given on page 48.

CLIMBING PLANTS FOR ARCHES AND PERGOLAS

H ere is a selection of plants to supply every intensity of colour, inebriating scent and velvety texture. Some flowers hang in falling sprays, others have trailing tresses, a few ripen into glittering pendulous bunches of fruit. To walk among and beneath such plants is a dream-like experience.

Yet gardening is a practical craft and one in which common sense is as vital as artistry.

One needs plants one can do business with. In consequence, ease of culture, adaptability and freedom from disease is as important as a beautiful appearance. I give a warning in the following lists if a plant is particularly prone to trouble.

Roses

R oses are everyone's favourite for many combine perfume, depth of texture and a spectrum of colour for every planting scheme. Their simplicity of culture varies, however. In general, climbers are easier than ramblers:

they require less maintenance and they are also recurrent-flowering. (Present classification groups the non-recurrent summer-flowering climbers with ramblers.)

Of the two groups, ramblers look the more at ease on overhead structures because their natural laxness of growth – a drawback on a wall – turns itself into the virtue of pliancy on an arch etc. In this airy position, they are also less likely to be susceptible to mildew or blackspot. They have two disadvantages. Firstly, most flower once only (although this is no less than we tolerate from many other plants). The second is that they require annual pruning or cutting down to ensure

good growth for the following year. (Details are given on page 60).

The suitability of any rose to its position will depend on its growth and it is important to relate its height to your requirements. A good pillar rose of 6 – 8ft/1.8 – 2.4m will be no good if you want it to leap overhead and shower you with blossoms. With this rider in mind, any of the following ramblers (shown as R in the list), climbers (indicated by Cl) or shrubs (Sh) are suitable:

ABOVE: Rosa 'Climbing Iceberg' over a screen in a formal setting.

OPPOSITE: Bourbon rose 'Blairii No. 2'.

Roses of Vigorous Growth (more than 15ft/4.6m) for Pergolas or Large Structures

WHITE, CREAM OR BLUSH

Adelaïde d'Orléans (R) Raised in 1826 in France. Once-flowering in loose clusters of very pale blush blossoms that hang down, so ideal for an arch. Persistent leaves so may be evergreen in mild winters, but cut down in freezing ones. Growth to 20ft/6m.

Albéric Barbier (R) Small yellowish buds opening to creamy semi-double blossoms with a wonderfully fresh apple scent. Once-flowering but repeats. Tough in inhospitable conditions. Persistent foliage. 20ft/6m.

Climbing Iceberg (Cl) Large, luminous, semi-double white blooms carried in profusion over a long period – spectacular. 20ft/6m.

Félicité et Perpétue (R) Charming white very double rosettes set against dark shiny leaves. Profuse display in mid-summer. Tough and hardy but a disadvantage is that the flowers brown obtrusively when dying. 20ft/6m.

Madame Alfred Carrière (Cl) Large double flowers, suffused faintly with pink. Wonderful first flush, followed by a partial second flowering. Strong growth to 20ft/6m.

Paul's Lemon Pillar (Cl) Huge, memorable lemon-white flowers early and once only in the season. Strong scent. Can be leggy and is therefore better on a structure where it can be loosely trained into a fan to encourage flowering from further down. 20ft/6m.

Seagull (R) Once-flowering but a snowstorm of white single blossoms with golden stamens, presented in huge clusters. 20ft/6m.

PINK

Madame Grégoire Staechelin (Cl) Huge frilly rich pink flowers with heavy fragrance of sweet peas. Once and early flowering making unique display, followed by large yellowing hips. 20ft/6m.

May Queen (R) Charming lilac-pink, full double flowers with quartering opening from small buds. Very free-flowering though once-only. Good scent. Will tolerate chilly inhospitable positions. 20ft/6m.

Paul's Himalayan Musk (R) Of huge dimensions, so only for the largest structures over which it will pour showers of its pink

The rambler 'Adelaïde d'Orléans'.

intensely scented rosettes for a fortnight in summer. Nothing to equal its pink pendulous snowdrift. Rampant to 40ft/12m.

Princess Marie (syn. Reine des Belges) (R) Once-flowering but torrential display of pink, exquisitely-formed, double blooms held in pendent sprays. Sweet scent. 20ft/6m plus.

YELLOW OR BUFF

Alister Stella Gray (syn. Golden Rambler) (Cl) Tea noisette with deep yellow centred double flowers, paling at the edges. Recurrent bloom. Can be slow to start growing well. 15ft/4.6m.

Mermaid (Cl) Spectacular rose with large single sulphur yellow blossoms and amber stamens produced continuously after midsummer. Good glossy foliage, stout thorns and ruby re-growth. Vulnerable in severe winters in any but a sheltered position. Pruning not advisable, so only for structures where its spread is suitable. 30ft/9m.

APRICOT

Albertine (R) Ubiquitous, much-loved salmon pink and copper rose with long and prolific though once-flowering display. Good scent.

The tea rose 'Climbing Lady Hillingdon' has pendent heads that nod towards you.

Rather stiff growth for a rambler. Mildew can be a problem though less likely in an airy position. 15ft/4.6m.

Desprez à Fleure Jaune (Cl) A tea noisette with warm peach, double, quartered blossoms produced recurrently over a long period. Was there ever such a scent as this? Thin only in winter. 20ft/6m.

François Juranville (R) Large, loosely double, perfumed flowers of warm apricot, once-flowering, set against dark leaves. Long, pliant shoots so it is sometimes grown as a weeping standard. Higher quality than Albertine. 15ft/4.6m.

Lady Hillingdon (Cl) Climbing form of the rare tea-rose bush; apricot-yellow with sweet scent, and bronze young leaves. Good overhead because the full, double flowers are weak-stemmed so pendent. Long period of bloom, but needs shelter. 20ft/6m.

Red

Crimson Showers (R) Excellent subject as it blooms in later summer, with small double flowers of a glowing crimson, held in pendulous sprays. It is sometimes confused with Excelsa, but this has a white-centre to its flowers and is not so reliable. 15ft/4.6m.

Etoile de Hollande (Cl) Climbing sport of the hybrid tea, dark bright red, wonderful scent and a recurrent habit, sometimes even into late autumn. Slow, but then to 20ft/6m.

Purple/Mauve

Rose-Marie Viaud (R) A dark purple fading pale with small very double flowers, once-blooming and dark leaves. Stalks very prone to mildew though its colour makes this less obvious. Scentless and nearly thornless. 15ft/4.6m.

Veilchenblau (R) Confused, tired and emotional, lilac and rich reddish-purple, small, semi-double rosettes, very floriferous and long-flowering during its single period of bloom which is better if shaded from afternoon sun. Scented. Light green leaves and nearly thornless stems. 20ft/6m.

Violette (R) Trusses of small double blossoms held in sprays, flowering once early to mid-season, opening dark crimson-purple and fading to grey and lilac. Scentless and virtually thornless. 15ft/4.6m.

'Gloire de Dijon': an old climber, sometimes prone to blackspot, but so lovely, so finely quartered and fragrant that it is still worth growing. It can be leggy in which case plants can be grown over its stems.

Less Vigorous Roses for Arches and Pillars (8ft/2.4m – 15ft/4.6m).

WHITE

Aimée Vibert (Cl) Clusters of double white and fragrant flowers, recurrent, and glossy dark leaves on rather lax growth. 12ft/3.6m.

Blush Noisette (Cl) A little charmer with a history and painted by Redouté. Clusters of pendent clove-scented small double flowers, presented in delicate falling sprays. Good pillar rose or for a little arbour. Continuously recurrent. 10ft/3m.

Sanders' White (R) Cascading clusters of small flowers, scented and very floriferous once and late in the season. Bright green foliage. 14ft/4m.

PINK

Aloha (Cl) Usually grown as a shrub but an adaptable climber for a short pillar with large rich pink blossoms, stuffed thickly with petals, well scented. Continuous flowering. 10ft/3m at most.

Blairii No. 2 (Sh) Bourbon rose which makes a beautiful opulent climber of deep pink, fading palely at the edges. Double heavily scented large blooms produced repeatedly. 12ft/3.6m.

Complicata (Sh) Gallica rose which will climb. Large single bright pink flowers with a white centre. Once flowering, making a tremendous show. 10ft/3m.

Constance Spry (Sh) Better as a lavish climber than a shrub, as the huge, richly scented,

luxuriant double blossoms need their stems
supported. Once-flowering. May be black-
spotty. 15ft/4.6m.

Debutante (R) Soft pink clusters of small
double flowers held in sprays. Once-
flowering but prolific and perfumed.
Somewhat like 'Dorothy Perkins' but far
lovelier colour and not subject to mildew.
Good foliage. Prune old flowering shoots from
the base immediately after they have
blossomed to encourage new growth the
following year. 13ft/4m.

New Dawn (Cl) Silver-pink double recurrent
blossoms, scented of apples, against shiny
healthy foliage. Reliable and a first choice.
12ft/3.6m.

Yellow/Buff

Emily Gray (R) A wonderful buff-yellow
semi-double rose, fragrant and usually once-
flowering though with the odd blossom later
in the year. Densely foliaged, the leaves are
red in youth, healthy and glossy dark green in
maturity. 15ft/4.6m.

Gloire de Dijon (Cl) Old and a bit prone to
black spot, but still very lovely. Full double
peachy yellow flowers, quartered and heavily
fragrant, repeating throughout the season.
Can be leggy so stems need covering with
other plants. 12ft/3.6m.

Goldfinch (R) Pretty yellow fading to white
flowers, scented, on smooth stems, in one
flush in summer. Graceful foliage. Not too
vigorous so good on a pillar or equivalent in
a yellow or blue colour scheme. 12ft/3.6m.

Leverkusen (Cl) Very hardy, with light yellow
double flowers which are very recurrent, a
good second flush coming in the autumn.
Light green leaves. 11ft/3.4m.

Apricot

Alchemist (Sh) Modern shrub rose which will
climb, in 'old-fashioned' style with fully
double flowers of warm yellow and orange,
scented, once-flowering; bronze young
leaves. Highly desirable. 12ft/3.6m.

Compassion (Cl) One of the best modern
roses, the climbing form of the hybrid tea,
making lots of growth from the base. Pale
pink to deep apricot-pink, scented and
recurrent. Dark, glossy leaves. 11ft/3.4m.

'Phyllis Bide' has recurrent flushes of bloom.

Phyllis Bide (R) Blooming into autumn with
scented soft yellow loosely semi-double little
flowers, flushed with pink, presented in
clusters. Good pillar rose. 10ft/3m.

Red
Parkdirektor Riggers (Cl) Velvet, bright deep
crimson single flowers in large clusters,
recurrently produced. Good dark green
foliage that covers the plants. Sometimes
tending to mildew. 12ft/3.6m.

Purple/Mauve
Bleu Magenta (R) The richest, deepest colour
of all the crimson-purples, becoming slate
purple in parts as the flowers age. Ravishing
but scentless. Once- and quite late-flowering.
Prune old shoots from their base. 12ft/3.6m.

Clematis

Clematis are frills and furbelows for the hardware of arches and pergolas. They are its fragile and flexible complement, disguising the legs, especially, of wooden and stone structures with their artless grace. Longer in flower than many other climbers and offering a season that stretches from spring until autumn, they are the great indispensables in this position. Many are too thin to be a substitute for other plants, but they are a necessary addition.

One special asset is that most clematis thrive as well and flower as profusely in a shady position as in sun, and may retain a better colour here. For this reason you can enjoy their flowers from the interior of a pergola. And see their blooms from nearby instead of at a distance overhead – though only a suitable variety and pruning will ensure this.

Clematis as Partners

Clematis are among the best companions for roses, scrambling around their ugly stems and smothering them politely with blossom. Both plants are greedy, however, so always provide every plant with plenty of planting space (a clematis needs a good 18in/45cm square and deep to itself) and feed each well.

You can select clematis to bloom before the rose, thereby filling an otherwise vacant flower slot. Or choose ones which bloom simultaneously with a rose to form the prettiest combinations: the blue 'Perle d'Azur' with the rose 'Crimson Showers' or C. viticella 'Etoile Violette' with the primrose blooms of the rose 'Mermaid'. Otherwise, later-flowering clematis can take the stage for themselves, after an earlier display by a plant like laburnum. In this case you are using the laburnum as an inert framework, a mere host for the clematis. A cultivar like the pink 'Comtesse de Bouchaud' will perform as memorably in late summer as her golden predecessor earlier in the year, giving you two different displays in the same area.

Wilt

Wilt is a common problem with clematis – the sudden death of shoots that have started to climb with thrilling vigour. It affects especially the large-flowered hybrids and usually in youth. It is because of wilt that you must plant a clematis 2in/5cm deeper in the ground than the soil in its container, burying its stem. This encourages it to put out replacement shoots in the event of trouble. Thorough and regular watering also helps to keep wilt at bay.

If it still strikes: a) cut the affected stem to the ground and burn, keep the roots moist and continue to feed; b) if the problem is general and recurrent, spray the clematis with Benlate or a suitable systemic fungicide in spring, autumn and at intervals throughout the summer, drenching the bottom 2-3ft/60-90cm of the stem; c) as a last resort confine yourself to the species that are resistant to wilt (avoiding the large-flowering hybrids). This said, one often finds that these hybrids will resist for no obvious reason in one position and not in another.

Finally, always plant clematis so that their roots are shaded by another plant, paving stones, chippings or a very thick mulch.

Clematis Varieties

In the following lists, pruning codes A, B, C and D are given. For A, thin end shoots and tidy the plant lightly to the main framework after flowering. For B, in late winter/early spring, cut back by one-third all the growth made in the previous year. For C, in late winter/early spring, cut back all the previous year's growth to 1ft/30cm of the base. For D, no pruning needed unless the clematis is overflowing its space. Often pruning is optional and you can adapt it to encourage flowering at a suitable height or time.

WHITE
C. armandii (D) Cascading clusters of small blush-white waxen and scented flowers in spring. Evergreen trifoliate leaves. Lovely for a large structure. 20ft/6m.

Clematis for Arches and Pergolas

C. florida **'Sieboldii'** (D) Creamy 3in/7.5cm
flowers with a boss of purple stamens in
summer. Very beautiful, tricky and needs
pampering on a warm wall as possible arbour
material. 6ft/1.8m.

Huldine (C) Translucent pearly white, mauve
shadowed on the reverse, flowers from
summer till autumn. Good foliage. Very
desirable. 15ft/4.6m plus.

C. jouiniana **'Praecox'** (C or optional) Semi-
herbaceous with foam of bluish-white tiny
flowers in late summer-autumn. Lovely
entwined with purplish-red *C. viticella*
varieties. 12ft/3.6m.

Madame Le Coultre (syn. Marie Boisselot) (A
if necessary) Very large blooms of great purity
and fine formation in high summer. Leathery
foliage. 12ft/3.6m.

C. montana grandiflora (A) Late spring/early
summer-flowering with 3in/7.5cm pure white
scented blooms. Exquisite spangling effect in
shade but only for very large structures.
25ft/7.6m.

C. viticella **'Alba Luxurians'** (C) Mass of
white, sometimes green-tipped twisted
flowers with dark anthers late summer
onwards. 10ft/3m plus.

ABOVE: Clematis 'Etoile Violette' and the rose
'Mermaid'.

BELOW: Clematis florida 'Sieboldii'.

49

PINK

Comtesse de Bouchaud (C) Large lilac-pink blossoms with cream stamens from late summer to autumn, very free-flowering and vigorous. A first choice. 10ft/3m.

Hagley Hybrid (C) Free-flowering, soft pink with brown stamens. Continuously from summer to autumn. Best in shade. 7ft/2.1m.

C. macropetala 'Markham's Pink' (D) Small, nodding double flowers in spring of lavender-pink with cream stamens. One of the enchanters. 10ft/3m.

C. montana rubens (D) Pale lilac-pink lightly scented 2in/5cm flowers in late spring, slightly bronzed young foliage. Vigorous; only for large structures. 25ft/7.6m.

C.m. 'Tetrarose' (D) 3in/7.5cm flowers of rosy-mauve and bronzed green foliage. Effective on a large structure. 20ft/6m.

Nelly Moser (D) Ubiquitous cultivar but good here as it will retain the colour of its large, lilac-pink, carmine-barred flowers better in shade. Early summer. 10ft/3m.

BLUE OR LAVENDER-BLUE

C. alpina 'Frances Rivis' (D) Small, drooping, lantern-shaped blue flowers with white petaloid stamens in spring. 7ft/2.1m.

Ascotiensis (C) Bright blue large flowers with green stamens produced continuously from summer till autumn. 10ft/3m.

Barbara Jackman (A or D) Blue sepals with a petunia bar and cream stamens in early summer. Better in some shade. 10ft/3m.

C. × durandii (C) Semi-herbaceous species with unique indigo deeply channelled ribs and white stamens in summer till autumn. Excellent for a pillar or for hiding legs and stems. 6ft/1.8m.

Elsa Spath (Optional) Large violet-blue flowers with dark stamens. Continuous, lovely, reliable. 8ft/2.4m.

Lasurstern (D) Very large lavender-blue showy flowers with cream stamens in early summer. 10ft/3m.

C. macropetala (D) Very beautiful nodding semi-double flowers in spring and dissected foliage. 'Maidwell Hall' is an exceptionally fine intense blue form. 10ft/3m.

Perle d'Azur (C) A profusion of large sky-blue flowers with green stamens from summer

Clematis 'Vyvyan Pennell', the best of the double-flowered cultivars.

until autumn. 12ft/3.6m plus.

Vyvyan Pennell (D) The best double clematis: lavender rosette with golden stamens in early summer, some single flowers later. 10ft/3m.

DEEP VIOLET-PURPLE

Gipsy Queen (C) Rich colour, velvet-textured free-flowering and vigorous with reddish-purple stamens. Late summer till autumn with great continuity. 15ft/4.6m plus.

Jackmanii Superba (C) Deep velvety purple with green stamens: the sepals are slightly broader than those of 'Jackmanii'. Prolific from summer until autumn. 15ft/4.6m plus.

Lady Betty Balfour (C) An autumn bloomer, so it must be in full sun to flower. Massed with large violet-blue blossoms with yellow stamens. 15ft/4.6m plus.

Clematis 'Comtesse de Bouchaud', still flowering madly in autumn on a pergola.

Clematis 'Niobe', the finest of the red clematis; it has deep velvety blooms.

C. viticella **'Etoile Violette'** (Optional) Larger flowers than usual for a *viticella*. Deep purple, 3in/7.5cm wide with yellow anthers, flowering summer till autumn. 12ft/3.6m.

C.v. **'Polish Spirit'** (Optional) Wonderful clouds of rich reddish-violet small blossoms in late summer until autumn. 12ft/3.6m.

C.v. **'Purpurea Plena Elegans'** (Optional) Unique variety with small very double reddish purple rosettes in a non-stop display from summer until autumn. Needs a pale background or plant as a foil. Desirable. 12ft/3.6m.

C.v. **'Royal Velours'** (Optional) The deepest velvet purple of all the *viticella* varieties, flowering summer until autumn. A great beauty which needs to be seen nearby. 12ft/3.6m.

CRIMSON

Niobe (B) The highest quality of all the large-flowered reds. Velvet, garnet flowers with yellow stamens, long in bloom. 8ft/2.4m.

Ville de Lyon (C) Best in some shade as the flowers can bleach from their carmine. Good continuity of flower from early summer (if left unpruned) to autumn. 10ft/3m.

C. viticella **'Abundance'** (Optional) Clouds of flowers like tiny wine-red butterflies in late summer until autumn. 12ft/3.6m plus.

C.v. **'Kermesina'** (Optional) Burgundy velvet flowers 3in/7.5cm across from summer until autumn. A beauty. 10ft/3m.

C.v. **'Madame Julia Correvon'** (C) 3in/7.5cm wine-red sepals which are twisted and widely spaced, with golden stamens from summer until autumn. 7ft/2.1m.

Lonicera periclymenum *'Belgica'* is extremely floriferous and fragrant in early summer.

Climbers in Variety

Aristolochia durior (syn. *A. sipho*, *A. macrophylla*) is called the Dutchman's Pipe because of the oddly shaped 1in/2.5cm buff flowers in summer. It is grown for its foliage, however. It will do a fast and complete smothering job on a large, stout structure. The size of its light green leaves varies according to the quality of the soil. In good rich ground, expect up to 10in/25cm in the shape of an elongated heart. Provide wires which will give its twining stems direction. 20ft/6m.

Akebia quinata Vigorous with fresh green foliage composed of five leaflets on a single stalk, yellowing prettily in autumn. 4in/10cm racemes of dusky purple-maroon flowers in spring are followed after a hot summer by violet-grey sausages, splitting to show black seeds in a white pulp. 20ft/6m.

***Campsis × tagliabuana* 'Madame Galen'** The best of the campsis for general use, with large salmon-red clusters of trumpets. Needs a hot sheltered position but even then can be late into leaf, though its pinnate foliage, nicely yellow in autumn, is one of its big assets. For large pergolas. 20ft/6m.

***Humulus lupulus* 'Aureus'** Prodigiously fast herbaceous perennial with lime-gold leaves fading unless planted in sun or very light shade. Brilliant effect and needs chosen companions. The blue clematis 'Perle d'Azur' would be lovely. 15ft/4.6m.

Hydrangea petiolaris Charming quiet

Hydrangea petiolaris.

scrambler, slow at first, with large corymbs of creamy lace-cap flowers in summer, whose skeletons remain long after blooming. It climbs by attaching itself with aerial roots but will need to be tied to some kind of framework initially. Good tall pillar subject over which it will mound. Shade tolerant. 20ft/6m.

Jasminum officinale Sprays of tiny white intensely fragrant flowers from midsummer to early autumn against dark pinnate leaves. 25ft/7.6m. There are also white and golden variegated forms (*J.o.* 'Argenteum' and *J.o.* 'Aureum') which are less vigorous (to 10ft/3m) and require a sheltered position. Good for pillars over which it can twine, given a wire framework.

J. × stephanense is a hybrid with pale pink clusters of scented flowers which would make a delicately pretty pillar. This will grow to about 10ft/3m.

Lathyrus latifolius (Everlasting Pea) Lovely cottage subject making a suitable climbing perennial for pillars, arches, pergola uprights, where it should be tied to wires or allowed to ramble through trellises. The type has rose pink shaded flowers from summer to autumn, but there is a lovelier glistening white form of great purity. This needs sun; the pink form is more shade-tolerant. Annual growth to 8ft/2.4m.

Lonicera in variety (Honeysuckle) Scent and abundant flowers make honeysuckles one of the prime plants for structures. In these airy positions, they are also less likely to become infested with aphids. The best include L. × *americana*, making a great early summer canopy of yellow and purple flowers, 20ft/6m high; L × *etrusca* 'Superba', growing to 12ft/3.6m with creamy-yellow intensely fragrant flowers from late summer to early autumn; L. *periclymenum* 'Belgica' '(early Dutch honeysuckle) with deep purple-red fading to yellow-red inflorescences in early summer and L.p. 'Serotina' (Late Dutch) from summer until autumn, both 12ft/3.6m. Think twice before succumbing to the coppery L. × *tellmaniana* and the lemon L. *tragophylla*, both highly glamorous plants for shade, but scentless.

Parthenocissus henryana Lovely ornamental vine with silver-veined, dark green, three- or five-lobed leaves. These bronze in summer, becoming maroon and ruby in autumn. Plant near late flowers such as the white *Clematis viticella* 'Alba Luxurians'. 10ft/3m plus.

Passiflora caerulea The passion flower is a woody climber which may act as a perennial after a severe winter. For distinction and mass-flowering, it is hard to excel, its 4in/10cm white flowers, bossed with blue filaments, studding the plant all summer. The ivory 'Constance Elliott' is a marvellous form. New mauve hybrids are also appearing on the market but their hardiness is not fully tested. Give it full sun, shelter and tie it to wires or a trellis. 15ft/4.6m.

Solanum crispum 'Glasnevin' Blue-violet yellow-beaked clusters of flowers sheet this plant on their first eruption in early summer and continue without check until autumn. Vigorous, but it is not a true climber and needs tying to wires or trellis. Lovely with pink/mauve clematis like 'Nelly Moser' or a later cultivar such as 'Comtesse de Bouchaud'. Full sun. 10ft/3m.

Solanum jasminoides 'Album' Rather tender and must have full sun and shelter, preferably against a wall in less mild regions, where it will produce its clusters of white fleshy stars with golden beaks from summer until autumn. Will twine itself around wires (or plants), but needs to be anchored when young. 12ft/3.6m.

Vitis 'Brandt' (*Vitis vinifera* 'Brant') The best colouring grapevine, its five-fingered light green leaves turning ruby and orange in autumn when its pendent bunches of purple-black grapes ripen. Lovely subject for a screen or pergola. Tie its heavy branches to anchor points though its tendrils will twine indiscriminately. 20ft/6m.

Vitis coignetiae A complete and vigorous foliage job (though deciduous) for a large structure you are ashamed of. Up to 12in/30cm furrowed green leaves, brilliant crimson in autumn, especially memorable with silver underplanting. It is not self-clinging; tie it to wires, though its tendrils will give it some support. 30ft/9m.

Vitis vinifera 'Purpurea' Less vigorous than the type, this beautiful grapevine turns gradually from soft sage green on unfurling to dusty purple in late summer and eventually to near-black. Well partnered with a carmine clematis like 'Ville de Lyon'. Stubby clusters of black grapes in autumn which are too bitter to eat raw but delicious as a jelly. 15ft/4.6m.

Wisteria floribunda My own first choice for any pergola or stout arcade. Weeping racemes up to 2ft/60cm of pea-flowers, lilac and white, fragrant, dizzyingly beautiful in the mass. The white form W.f. 'Alba' is wondrous. 'Macrobotrys' has even longer mauve pendants, but these may be inconvenient, catching in one's hair as one walks beneath. Also, it suffers to a greater degree from the fact that the flowers at the top of the raceme decay before the bottom ones open. Full sun. 20ft/6m.

Wisteria sinensis The Chinese wisteria is the more frequently seen and has shorter racemes but is almost as lovely. Very good forms include the deep-blue scented 'Caroline' and the double dark purple 'Black Dragon'. 'Prematura Alba' is an early-flowering white form. Full sun. 40ft/15m.

Trees or Shrubs

Laburnum × watereri 'Vossii' The tunnel subject, where a tree is planted each side to meet in the centre. 12in/30cm long racemes of golden pea flowers in later spring/early summer and trifoliate leaves. Of vigorous growth, it can make an effective tunnel within six years. Prune dead or excess growth replace with new suitable shoots for quality flowers.

Robinia hispida 'Rosea' This pinnate-leafed tree is always grafted as it suckers on its own roots. Its stubby pink racemes are as abundant in summer as a wisteria's, and stray blossom also appear in autumn. An outright beauty for arches or arcades, one planted to each leg of the support. Not always as easy as the laburnum to establish but it is worth any effort to try. Can be kept quite small. Full sun. 18ft/5.5m.

Tree Fruit

Apples or pears are normally chosen for tunnels (see page 37) and planted in pairs of the same variety. To ensure a crop of fruit, either the variety chosen must be self pollinating or, if sterile, different varieties must be planted as companions to secure cross-pollination. Always check this in advance with a reliable nurseryman. It is usual for the cordon fruit to be grown on the semi-dwarfing rootstock MM106. A large tunnel could also support one of the taller crab apples such as 'John Downie' which has naturally elongated growth, but one might well tire of apple jelly.

OPPOSITE: Wisteria floribunda 'Alba'.

HEDGING PLANTS FOR ARCHES AND ARBOURS

*I*n practice, any hedge that makes a hardy framework for a garden can be trained to form an arch. This is subject, however, to three restrictions. First, it would be folly to choose the kind of vigorous plant that requires clipping more than once a year: overhead training with hedge-clippers is amongst the most onerous of garden tasks. Second, arches and arbours are ornamental, even pompous, features. The material (i.e. the plants) from which they are formed should deserve the admiration they command. The third point concerns arches rather than arbours. Since they are usually part of the hedge, that same hedge (one assumes) has been chosen to fit the garden. This returns us to the key fact of arches etc: they must be part of the overall concept of the garden.

An evergreen arch or arbour might seem to have the edge over a deciduous one. It is there all the year, providing a fully-clothed frame. Looked at from the opposite point of view, this can become boring compared with the varied cycle of deciduous shrubs.

Tapestry arch with copper beech for contrast

Main Varieties

Beech (*Fagus sylvatica*) This makes the most handsome formal feature but it is not reliable on heavy wet soils, where it is subject to disease. Its fresh green leaves turn russet in autumn and, if the hedge is clipped annually in late summer, will stay on the plant throughout the winter. This means that the plant, though deciduous, continues to function as a screen. Copper beech is sometimes used either on its own or to give variegation to the type, but it needs careful placing.

Holly Only suitable for an arch (let alone arbour) if you select a virtually spineless cultivar such as *Ilex* × *altaclarensis* 'Camellifolia'. Its shiny evergreen leaves would make a polished feature. In severe continental climates, not all the evergreen hollies are dependably hardy but the *Ilex meservae* group of blue hollies, bred in America, are amongst the best for these conditions and 'Blue Stallion' and 'Blue Princess', planted together, will produce an abundant crop of berries. Spiny unfortunately.

Hornbeam *Carpinus betulus* is an unsurpassed deciduous tree for forming strong dense tunnels, arbours and stilt hedges, and it is more resistant to disease than beech. It too retains its withered leaves throughout the winter in a shade of donkey brown. One clip in late summer.

The hornbeam hedge at Birr Castle, Ireland; it is trimmed into an airy arcade.

Lime Most commonly used for pleached hedges as their supple branches lend themselves to this form of training. The commonest planted variety, *Tilia europaea* (*T. vulgaris*) is blemished by bushy growths and dense suckers. This disfigurement is less apparent on the large-leafed lime, *T. platyphyllos*, and not at all on the small-leafed lime, *T. cordata*. Annual clip in late summer. All are fully deciduous.

Yew *Taxus baccata* is the king, giving a distinguished and antique air to its surroundings, the perfect velvety background to flowers and making an unequalled subject for architectural topiary. Its tiny needle-like leaves and plush density of growth result in a precision of outline after clipping: the perfect pediment, angle, or image is obtainable. it will put on about 12in/30cm a year if grown in a sunny position in rich, regularly fed soil which is never waterlogged. 'Hicksii', a hybrid raised from *T. × meadia*, is one of the hardiest cultivars in the severest conditions, and has more upright growth than *T. baccata*. Yew cannot be planted where stock can reach it, as it is toxic to some animals and fowl.

Thuja occidentalis and ***T. plicata*** Both are very hardy evergreen conifers with glossy green leaves resembling cypress foliage, though with a distinctly orange scent if crushed. They can be trained to shape a neat thin close-textured form. Clip in late summer but allow the leader to reach the required height before cutting it.

Clematis jouiniana 'Praecox' is grown to mingle with C. viticella 'Purpurea Plena Elegans'. They are trained over a wide-gauge wire mesh which they will cover completely in due course. Both plants are pruned simultaneously in early spring.

PLANTING AND TRAINING

No climber will thrive unless it is given a sound start. It is astonishing that people sometimes plant two climbers in the same hole beside a pergola upright, and turn their back on the inevitable fight that ensues underground for available room, food and moisture. Always give a plant its own large hole, filled with compost and a sprinkling of fertilizer like blood, fish and bone; spread its roots out and water it in, firming the soil gently around it. Clematis need special treatment, whereby you bury their stems about 2in/5cm or more below the ground (see page 48).

Where you are planting against a wall or at the foot of a brick or stone upright, make sure you position the plant at least 12 – 18in/30 – 45cm away (and on the outside of a pergola), otherwise it can suffer from drought. Both the footings and the rain shadow caused by the wall or by an overhang from the canopy on a pergola can rob the plant of moisture, so it is wise to water and mulch it in later life too.

Right: Clematis grown over a post of angle irons to give height in a border.

Training Climbers

Climbers will flower more profusely and more evenly if you can fan out the shoots against a support rather than bunch them together like a rocket. This is easily achieved if you have linking material along the sides of your structure, like trellis. Tendrils or self-adhesive pads will cling to this, and you can tie in shoots that aren't self-supporting.

If you are growing your climber beside an upright, you will simplify training, if you cover the upright with a wide-meshed sleeve of netting to which you can tie the stems. With a flimsy plant, this can look obtrusive, in which case single wires encircling the upright like garters at 18in/45cm intervals will serve equally well. In any case, tie the climbing stems loosely to these to allow room for the plant to thicken without suffering constriction. Temporary ties can be of raffia, which will last a season, of string which will last a year, or of slivers of nylon stocking which has the advantage that it is expandable and won't chafe even when wind rocks the stems. Wire and even plastic-coated wire can do this.

Tying a plant into a structure organizes its shape and where its blooms appear. Without this, its shoots will fall down, scramble over other parts of itself or neighbours and become a tangled mat. This is often the case with clematis and you will have to continue to organize these over your canopy when they look as if they are running amok. The same is true of roses, of course, though always permit those with pendent flower stems to hang down. Several examples have been given in the plant lists: these have their own spraying beauty and must be given licence to show it off.

Roses with pliable stems can be wound round uprights in a spiral to check the flow of sap up the stem and encourage flowering along it.

59

Pruning

The more plants you grow on a structure, the stricter your pruning. If not, one plant will throttle another, an especially likely scenario if their rates of growth differ. Honeysuckle needs watching: it can spiral another plant in an iron grip. Wisteria also needs a firm hand; side shoots should be pruned back in summer to about four buds and the leaders will need shortening in winter when they have covered the required area.

Rambler roses should have their old stems cut out after they have flowered, allowing room for the new shoots to appear which will lengthen and flower the following season. The pruning of climbing roses is optional.

See page 48 for the key to pruning individual clematis, though remember you can alter the height a late-flowering clematis reaches the following season by the height at which you prune it the previous winter/spring.

Training Fruit Tunnels

The methods of training fruit trees for tunnels are labour-intensive but they do provide plenty of fruit in a limited space. It is usual to buy cordons on semi-dwarfing MM106 rootstock (this grows to about 15ft/4.6m), planting one to the foot of each rail, spaced at about 2½ft/75cm apart.

Very briefly, each new cordon will need notching in late spring to produce side shoots on the bare upper reaches and all the shoots should be pruned each summer to keep the tree productive later. Where lateral shoots grow directly from the main stem, they should be cut back to about 3in/7.5cm so that they form 'fruiting' spurs. Mature laterals are reduced in summer to three leaves (about 3 – 4in/7.5 – 10cm) beyond the basal cluster and those that arise from existing side shoots or spurs are cut back to one leaf (about 1in/2.5cm).

Espalier fruit can be grown equally well over ready-made tunnels which have horizontal wires running between its arches. You can buy fully trained espaliers from good nurseries, but it is cheaper to train a maiden (a one-year-old) yourself. Reduce this to 2–3in/5–7.5cm above the first horizontal wire of the tunnel, ensuring that there are three buds near the top where you are cutting. The top bud will lengthen to continue the main stem, and the lower two, each facing outwards, will be trained sideways along the wire to form the first tier of horizontal branches. Repeat this procedure each winter when the plant is dormant. When the espalier has filled its space and is established and fruiting, prune it only in summer as for the cordon, reducing the growth from the trunk and branches back to three leaves from the basal leaf cluster.

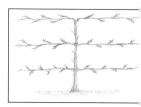

Espalier: in winter 2 sid *shoots are trained along th* *wire.*

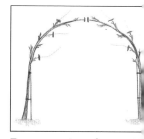

Trees on tunnel: remov *upright shoots. Cut back sid* *shoots to 3 buds. Cut leade* *as shown.*

Topiaried Arches

The principles for clip ping these are the sam as for hedges, aiming for dense, bushy structure. Allow the leaders of the bushe either side of your arch t grow on, over a frame necessary. Clip the side shoots lightly, but not the leaders or any part you wil use for your 'design'. Ther will be a long period durin which the two sides reach ou to each other before they joir up. You can hasten this by feeding the plants well, with quick-acting fertilizer once o twice in the summer and slow-acting one like bone meal in alternate autumns and make sure they are watered and mulched.

OPPOSITE: *Almost there.*

INDEX

PRINTED IN BELGIUM BY

INTERNATIONAL BOOK PRODUCTION